Presented to:

_____

Presented by:

_____

On this date:

_____

Why, Oh Why? Oh Me, Oh My!

Printed in the United States of America.
Published by Barbour and Company, Inc.
P.O. Box 719
Uhrichsville, Ohio 44683
ISBN 1-55748-651-4

WHY, OH WHY? OH ME, OH MY!
The Story of Job

A Barbour Book

"**H**ave you noticed my servant? He's gentle and kind
and our hearts are so sweetly, completely entwined.
He's as good as it gets. Yes, the cream of the crop.
The pick of the litter. The tip of the top!"

"And why not?" croaked the devil. "He's as rich as a king.
Why, you've never withheld even one little thing.
Take away all those whistles and hooters and bells
and I'll bet it's a whole different story he tells!"

Well, that night while Job snoozed in his big easy chair,
as he snurgled and snorgled, he got quite a scare.
Three men came abusting right into the room
and proceeded to fill him with gloom and with doom!

"Remember those hundreds of camels and sheep,
and the thousands of horses and donkeys you keep
in that field where you used to have millions of goats
by the lake where you always kept all of your boats,
and your barns and your pens and your coops and your stalls?
Well, some burglars came and they burgled it ALL!

But it doesn't end there 'cause those down-dirty stinkers
made off with your bangles and jingles and twinklers.
They snatched up your doodads and gizmos and blinkers!"

Poor Job was astounded. Completely dumbfounded!
His stomach glub-gurgled. His heart pumped and pounded.
But oh, don't you know, he got down on his knees.

He gave thanks to the Lord just as quick as you please!

"I just hate all that praising. It makes me quite ill!"
spat the devil. "But I can go one better still...
I'll give him some uh-ohs and boo-boos and stings!
Then I'll bet it's a whole different song that he sings!"

So Job became terribly, scare-ably sick.

He wheezled and woozled. He hacked and up-hicked!

"What good is your faith? It's a joke. It's a lie!

Give up!" Job's wife sputtered. "Just CURSE GOD AND DIE!"

"Curse God and die? Curse God and die!?

I cannot. I will not! But, why, oh Lord, WHY?"

News travels fast. Oh my yes, that's the truth!
And THIS news traveled straight to three friends from Job's youth
who took off right that minute, posthaste, P.D.Q.
to find out what was up, and see what they could do.

"It just isn't fair. No, it doesn't make sense.
This tragic, traumatical turn of events!
Lord, why be created, composed, or contrived
when I'm better not born, brought about, or alived!"

"Oh, give me a break!" Eliphaz blurted out.
"You've sinned a great sin. There can't be any doubt.
Just look at yourself. You're a mess! You're a wreck!
You've been up to no good, I suppose and suspect."

"Oh yes, we agree and as logic would show,
true enlightenment, knowledge, and learning, you know,
would have kept you from making that stupid mistake
of the kind and the type that we've known you to make."

"We KNOW that Job's utterly wicked and rotten,
but what does GOD think? That's the thing we've forgotten!
This punishment's awful. An outrage! A curse!
But it could have, and probably SHOULD have been worse!"

"What wonderful friends. What exquisite advice!
Did you say you were leaving? Yes, that would be nice!

I know that I'm righteous. I haven't a doubt.
My spirit is clean both within and throughout.
And although God destroys me and grinds me to dust,
it is Him whom I'll honor, abide in, and trust!

I've done nothing wrong. Yes, I KNOW that it's true.
So, tell me, Lord, **WHAT IN THE WORLD DID I DO?"**

"What did you do? Oh, if we only knew!"

"You must have been lying or cheating or stealing.
Yes, snitching and sneaking and squawking and squealing.
Oh, how could you do it? Oh, what did you do?
Oh, why are we standing here talking to you?!"

"Just who do you think that you're duping and fooling?
We're full of it, Job! Full of wisdom and schooling.
Go on," Bildad babbled, "rave, rant, roar, and hiss,
but remember, YOU got your own self into THIS!"

21

"Lord, why do You slay me? What gives You the right?
Has it done any good? Can it be Your delight?

You know that I'm righteous! I'm gentle and kind,
and our hearts are so sweetly, completely entwined.
Oh, why don't You answer? Oh, where is the man
who would bring us together? Send HIM, if You can!"

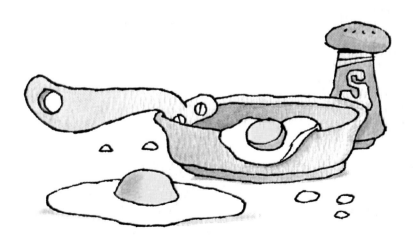

"Excuse me," said someone from back in the trees.
"Allow me to add my two cents, if you please:

These things I've been hearing!
These things you've been speaking!
This nonstop, right up to the eyeballs critiquing.
You speak against God. Boy, you've all got some guts!
What are you guys, crazy? What are you guys, nuts!?"

Well, those words weren't out of his mouth for one minute when the next thing I knew, we were standing there in it.

"Who filled up the oceans? Who turned on the stars?
Who brought forth Orion? The Milky Way? Mars?
Who made everything do the thing that it does?
Well I'll tell you: I did and I AM and I was!"

"Your home is with ME, Job. It isn't down here.

When all this is gone, all the why's and the how's,
all the to's and the fro's, all the here's and the now's,
there still will be you, and there still will be Me.
Together. Forever. Be patient. You'll see!"

Well, the Lord restored all of Job's cattle and goats,
his wife and his family, his friends and his boats.
And he lived to be more than one hundred and ten.
Very old. A bit wrinkled. Quite happy. Amen!